Scholastic Phonics

Unusual Structures

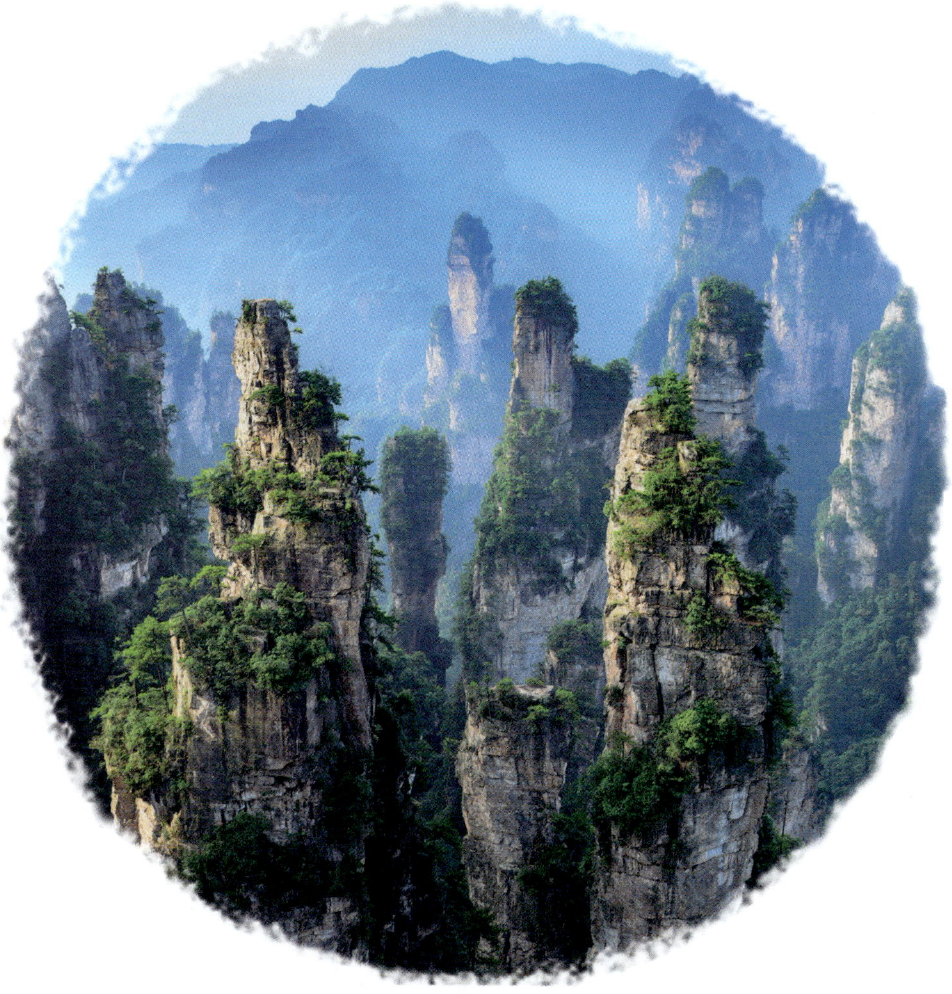

Published in the UK by Scholastic Education, 2023
Scholastic Distribution Centre, Bosworth Avenue, Tournament Fields, Warwick, CV34 6UQ
Scholastic Ireland, 89E Lagan Road, Dublin Industrial Estate, Glasnevin, Dublin, D11 HP5F

SCHOLASTIC and associated logos are trademarks and/or registered trademarks of Scholastic Inc.
www.scholastic.co.uk
© 2023 Scholastic
1 2 3 4 5 6 7 8 9   3 4 5 6 7 8 9 0 1 2

Printed by Ashford Colour Press
The book is made of materials from well-managed, FSC®-certified forests and other controlled sources.

A CIP catalogue record for this book is available from the British Library.
ISBN 978-0702-32118-4

All rights reserved. This book is sold subject to the condition that it shall not, by way of trade or otherwise, be lent, hired out or otherwise circulated in any form of binding or cover other than that in which it is published. No part of this publication may be reproduced, stored in a retrieval system, or transmitted in any form or by any other means (electronic, mechanical, photocopying, recording or otherwise) without prior written permission of Scholastic.

Every effort has been made to trace copyright holders for the works reproduced in this publication, and the publishers apologise for any inadvertent omissions.

Author
Giles Clare

Editorial team
Rachel Morgan, Vicki Yates, Gemma Smith, Jennie Clifford

Design team
Dipa Mistry, Andrea Lewis, We Are Grace

Photographs
Cover nycshooter/iStock
p4 RudiErnst/Shutterstock
p5 Kim Grosz/iStock
p6, 24 sculpies/iStock
p7 (Mexico pyramids) Prakich/iStock
p7 (glass pyramids) wolv/iStock
p3, 8 Monica Silva/iStock
p9 MediaProduction/iStock
p10, 24 tovfla/iStock
p11 ePhotocorp/iStock
p12 Aerial-motion/Shutterstock
p13, 24 (fabic dome) Chris Mansfield/iStock
p13 (steel and glass dome) Artur Bogacki/iStock
p14 (mansion) Jessica Kirsh/Shutterstock
p14 (treehouse) Daniel Lamborn/Shutterstock
p14 (unusual position) Nikola Spasic Photography/iStock
p15 (grassy village) mariusz_prusaczyk/iStock
p15 (mudbrick settlement) miroslav_1/iStock
p16 Mlenny/iStock
p17 (Italy) Alan_Tow/iStock
p17 (pagoda) AvigatorPhotographer/iStock
p18 Cristi Croitoru/iStock
p19 (mound) Binnerstam/iStock
p19 (chambers) frankix/iStock
p1, 20 (ice landscape) aphotostory/iStock
p20 (crystal ledges) prmustafa/iStock
p21 (waterfall) Rasmus Troell/Shutterstock
p21 (cave) CreativeMoments/iStock
p21 (lightbulb) VectorCookies/iStock
p22 (trees) Richie Chan/Shutterstock
p22 (maze) Wengen Ling/iStock
p23 (temple) Travel Wild/iStock
p23 (shipwreck) ultramarinfoto/iStock

Help your child to read!

This book practises these letters and letter sounds.
Point and say the sounds with your child:

gn (as in 'design')   kn (as in 'knows')   eer (as in 'engineers')
su (as in 'unusual')   dge (as in 'bridge')   ge (as in 'large')
y (as in 'pyramid')   ti (as in 'position')   si (as in 'mansion')
ci (as in 'ancient')

Your child may need help to read these common tricky words:

people   many   the   are   were   of
one   today   to   beautiful   through
do   any   into   because

Before reading
- Look at the cover picture and read the title together. Read the back cover blurb to your child.
- Ask your child: *What does your home look like? What is it made of? What is nearby?*
- Talk about the image in the magnifying glass.

During reading
- If your child gets stuck on a word, remind them to sound it out and then blend the sounds to read the word: p-y-r-a-m-i-d, pyramid.
- If they are still stuck, show them how to read the word.
- Enjoy looking at the pictures together. Pause to talk about the information.

After reading
- Talk about the images on page 24. What can your child tell you about them?
- Ask your child: *What is a dome? Where can you find pyramids? What shape would you make a skyscraper or a bridge?*
- Discuss your child's favourite structure. Ask them to explain why they like it.

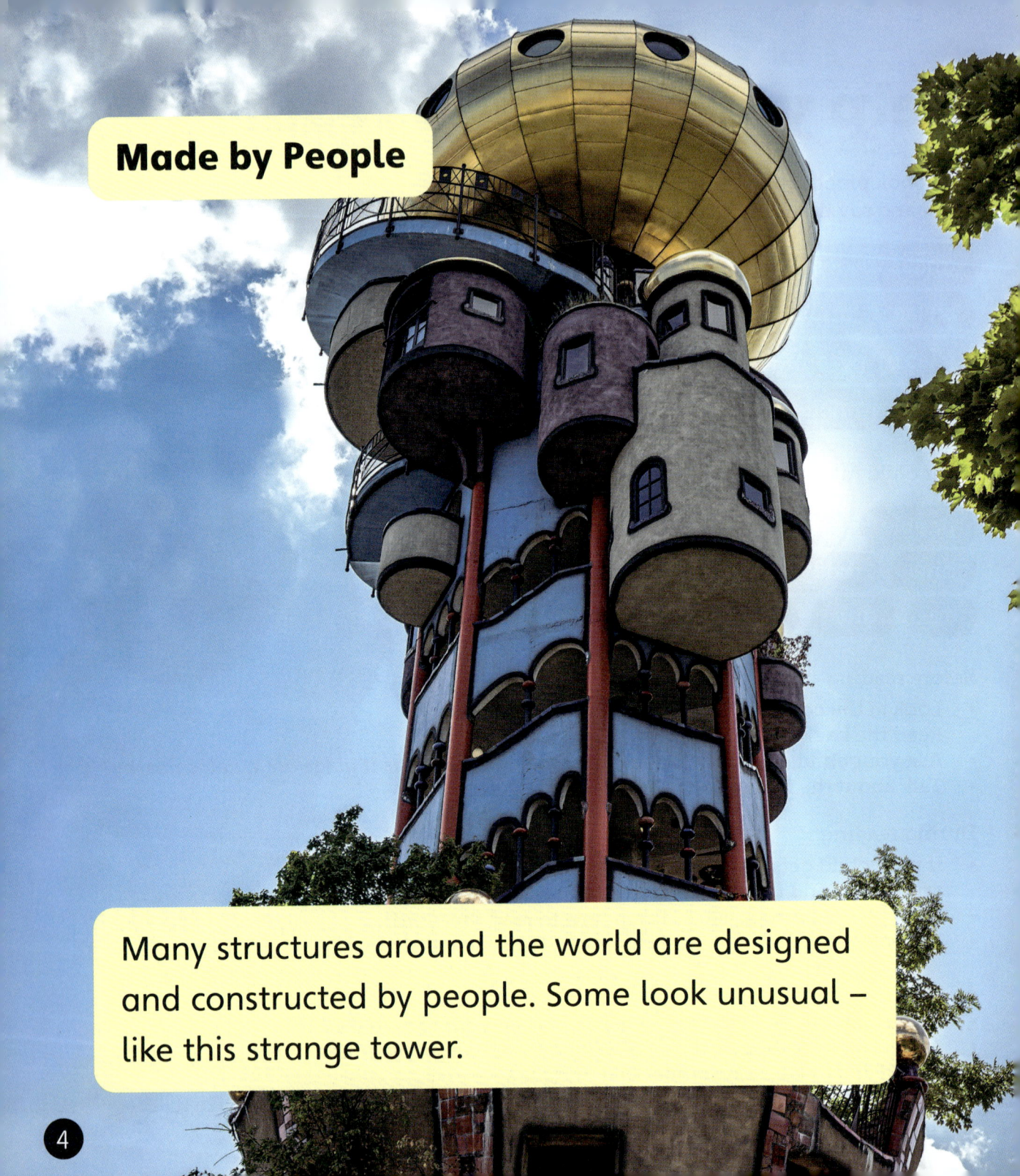

Made by People

Many structures around the world are designed and constructed by people. Some look unusual – like this strange tower.

Made by Nature

Nature also creates some unusual structures. These towers were formed by the motion of wind and water on the rock (erosion).

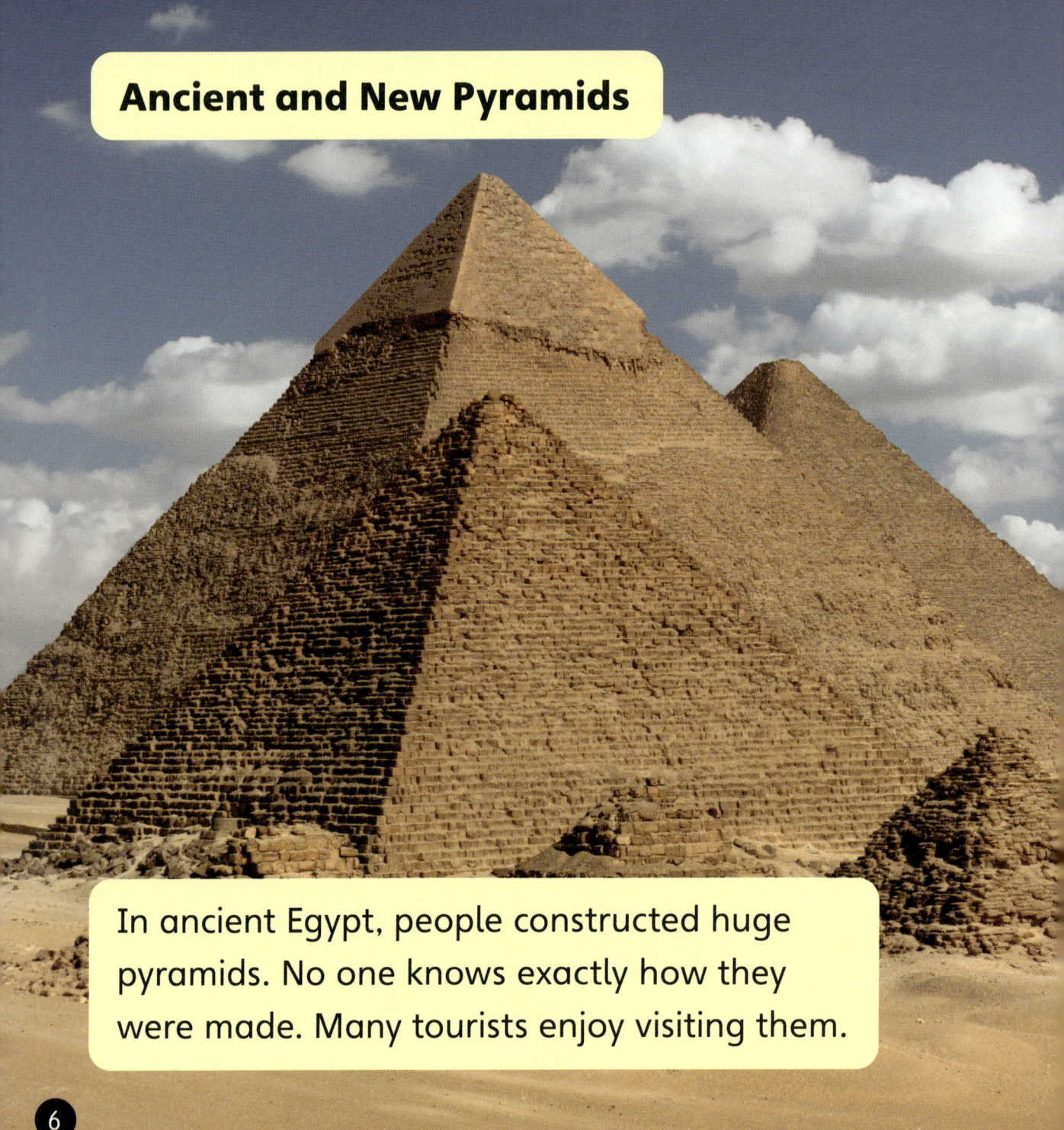

Ancient and New Pyramids

In ancient Egypt, people constructed huge pyramids. No one knows exactly how they were made. Many tourists enjoy visiting them.

More pyramids can be found across the world.

This collection of pyramids is in Mexico.

Engineers today know how to use glass to make pyramid structures. These were an extension to a museum.

Bridges

A bridge is used to cross an obstacle, like a river.

This beautiful old bridge in Italy crosses a canal and has shops on it.

Here is a suspension bridge over a gorge.
Would you look over the edge at the sheer drop?
Would you walk across the see-through floor?

This rock bridge was left behind when water, wind and frost made the weaker rock below the bridge collapse.

This suspension bridge in Asia is made from living tree roots! It may not look strong, but a bridge like this can hold a great weight.

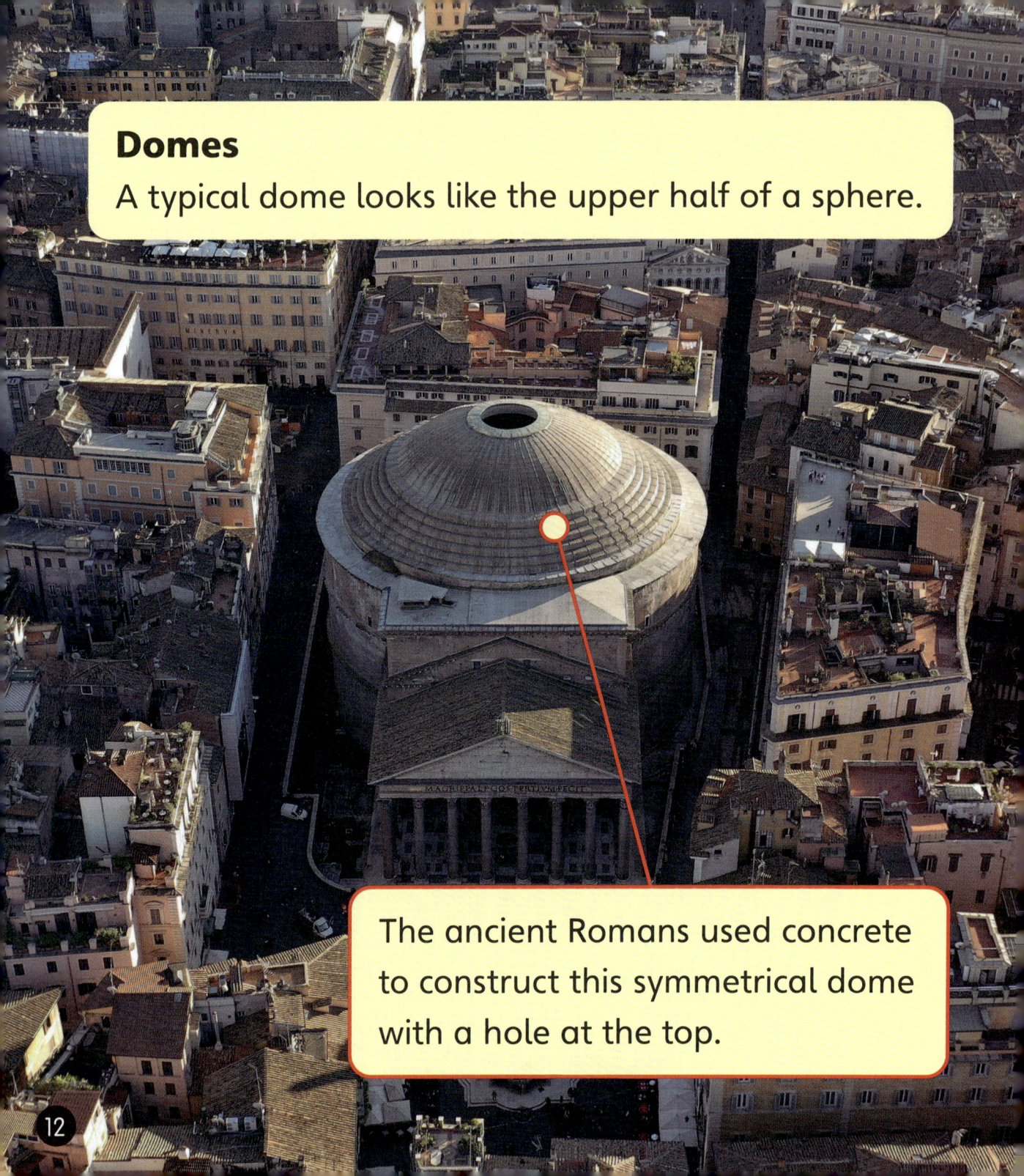

Domes

A typical dome looks like the upper half of a sphere.

The ancient Romans used concrete to construct this symmetrical dome with a hole at the top.

Today, designers and engineers have more options when they choose what to construct a dome from.

special lightweight fabric

steel and glass

Homes

Homes come in all shapes and sizes.

an unusual position

a rainforest treehouse

a spacious mansion

Do you know any homes with an unusual design?

a mudbrick settlement

a grassy village

Which of these homes would you like to live in?

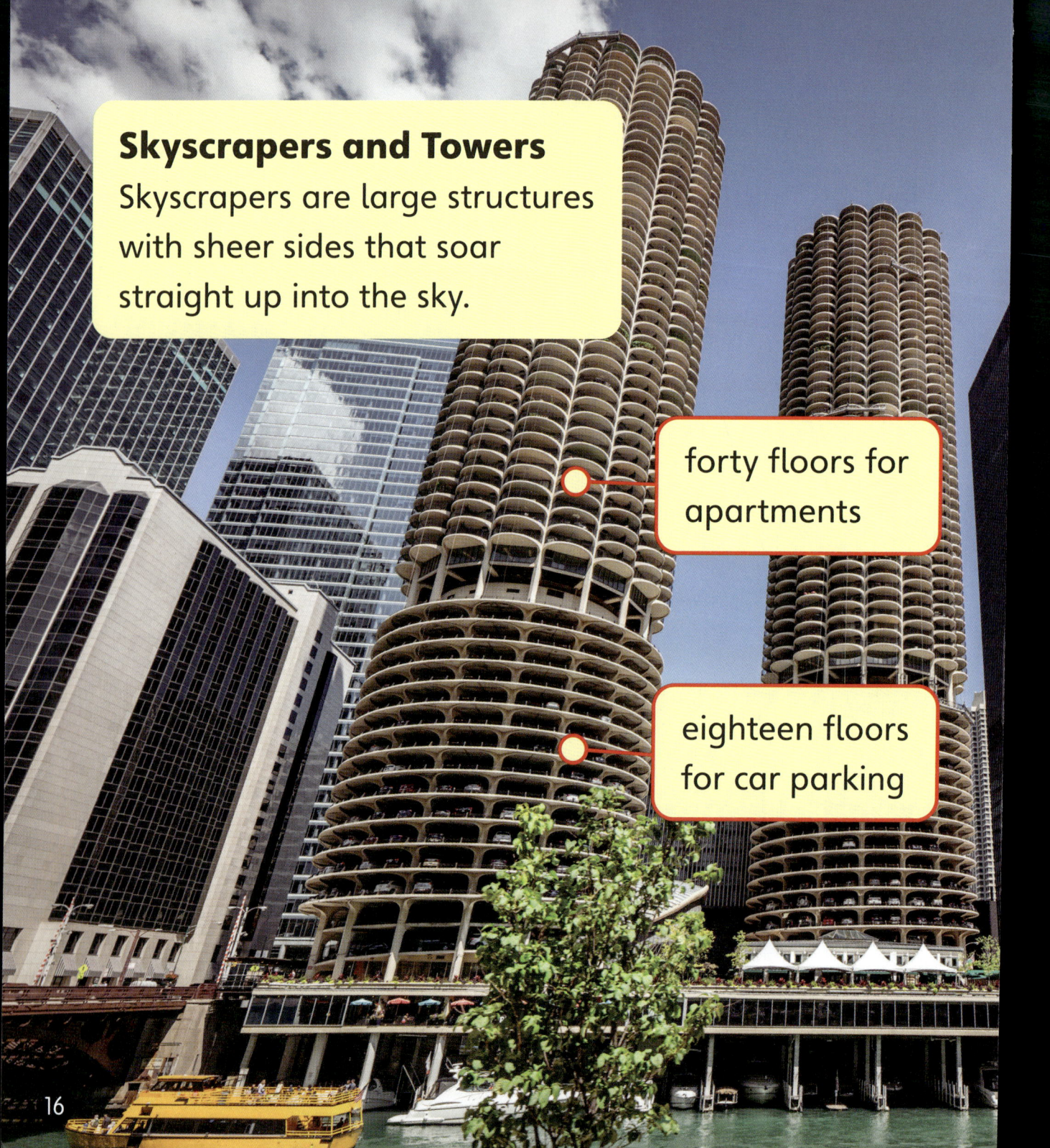

Skyscrapers and Towers

Skyscrapers are large structures with sheer sides that soar straight up into the sky.

forty floors for apartments

eighteen floors for car parking

These towers are old.

This tower in Italy is well known because it leans to one side.

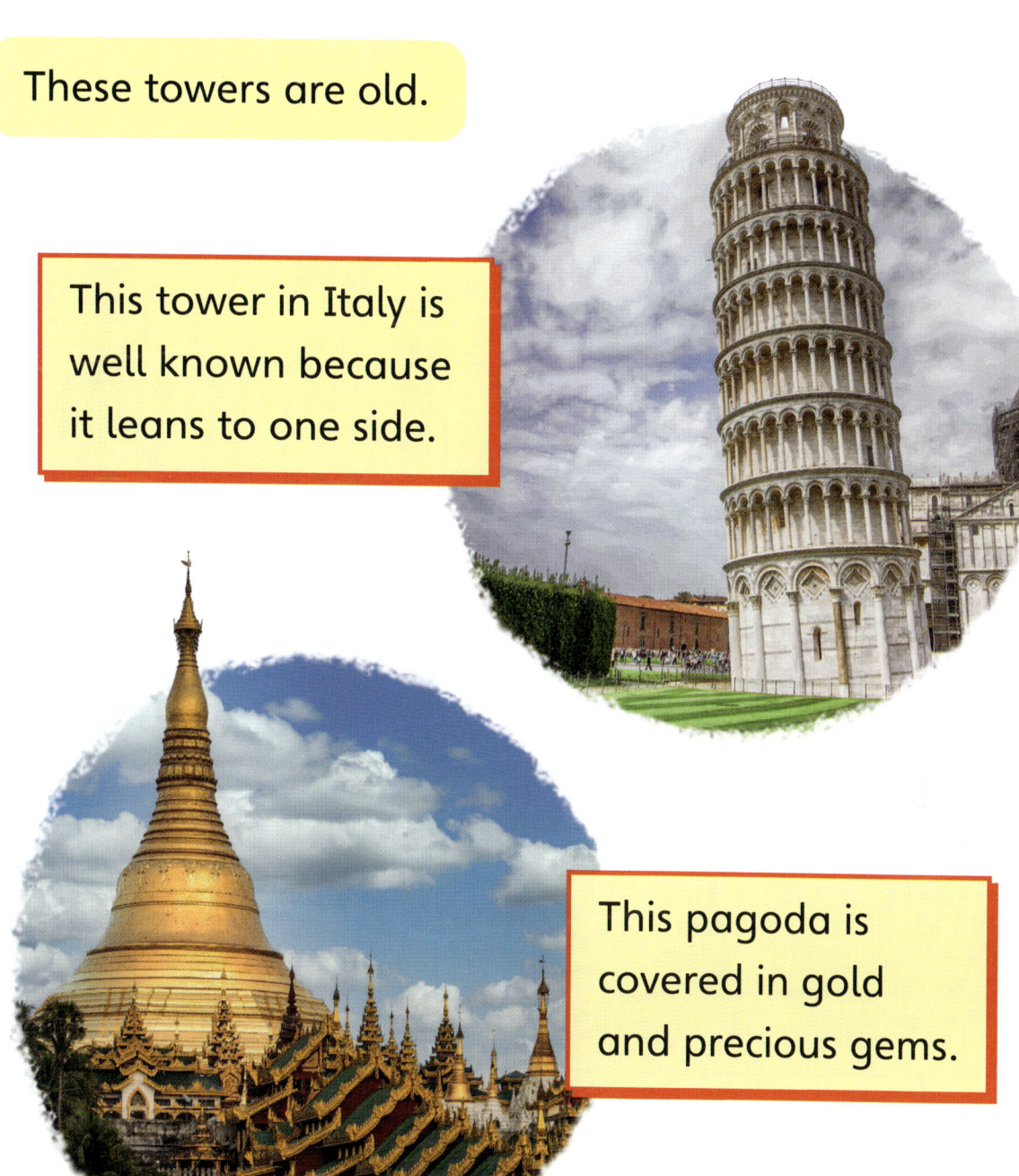

This pagoda is covered in gold and precious gems.

Places for the Dead
These structures were made as places to lay the dead to rest.

This monument was carved into the rock face to store an ancient king and his treasures.

Many of these places are found underground.

There may be a great ruler under this strange mound.

This is a system of underground chambers in Rome.

Nature's Wonders

Unusual structures can form where rock and water meet.

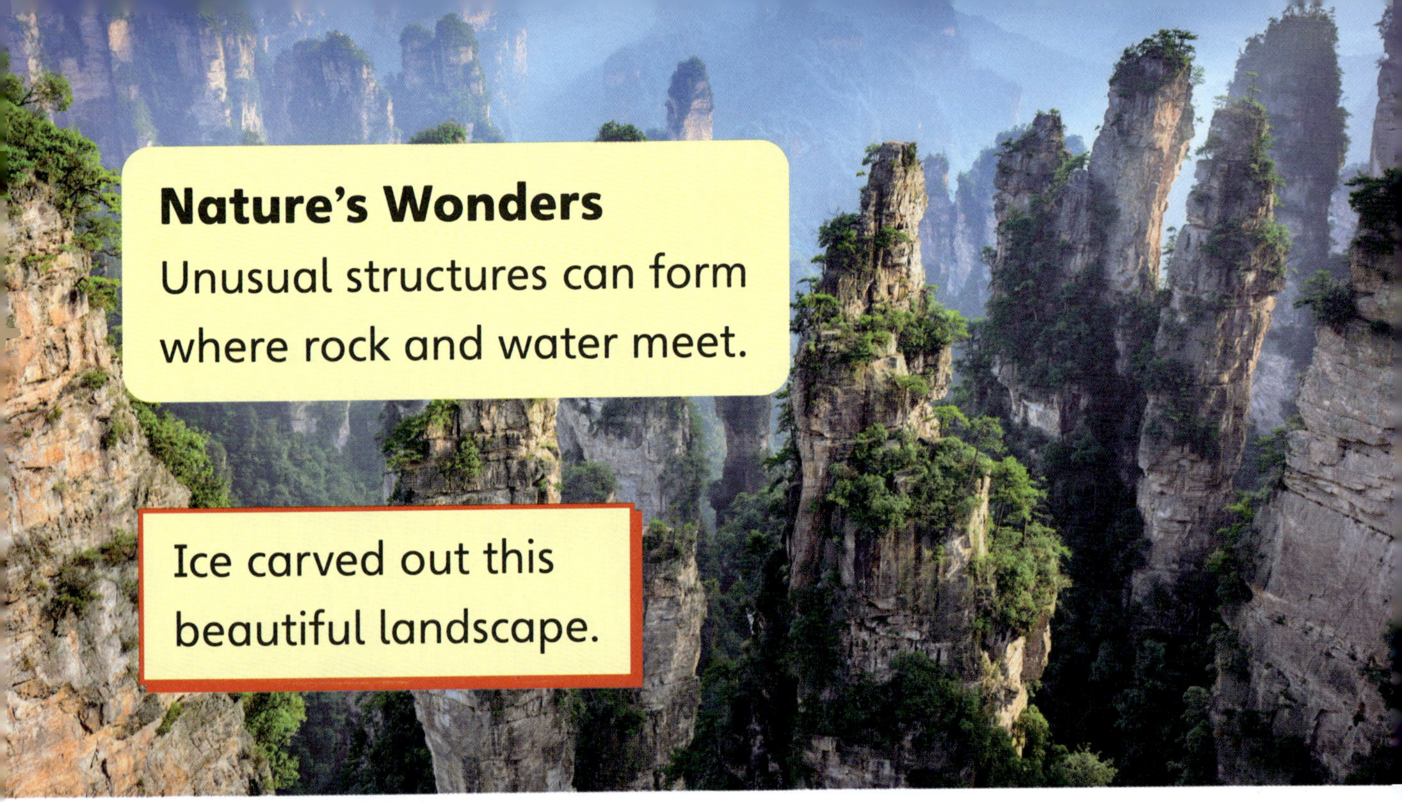

Ice carved out this beautiful landscape.

These crystal ledges were left by hot springs.

a frozen waterfall

This is a cave formed by an underground river.

💡 Glow-worms live in the cave and tourists travel by boat to see them.

Artificial Meets Nature

Sometimes people design structures using nature.

These artificial trees are made from metal and plants.

This garden maze is made from hedges.

Sometimes people leave structures behind. Then nature takes over!

A huge tree grows on this old temple.

This shipwreck is now home to coral and fish.

Talk about it!